THE CALL OF DUTY
CAREERS IN THE
ARMED FORCES™

YOUR CAREER IN
THE NAVY

TAMRA ORR

ROSEN
PUBLISHING®

New York

Published in 2012 by The Rosen Publishing Group, Inc.
29 East 21st Street, New York, NY 10010

First Edition

Library of Congress Cataloging-in-Publication Data

Orr, Tamra.
Your career in the Navy / Tamra Orr.—1st ed.
    p. cm.—(The call of duty : careers in the armed forces)
Includes bibliographical references and index.
ISBN 978-1-4488-5511-7 (library binding)
1. United States. Navy—Juvenile literature. 2. United
States. Navy—Vocational guidance—Juvenile literature. I.
Title.
VA55.O77 2012
359.0023'73—dc22

                                                    2011007017

Manufactured in the United States of America

CPSIA Compliance Information: Batch #W12YA: For further information, contact Rosen Publishing, New
York, New York, at 1-800-237-9932.

CONTENTS

INTRODUCTION

T he call came in out of the blue. On December 26, 2004, an earthquake had struck off the coast of Indonesia and a huge tsunami had slammed into the country's shore, killing thousands and wounding even more. Countless people were missing. Petty Officer John Armstrong was stationed on the USS *Abraham Lincoln* in Hong Kong when the news arrived. Originally from Portland, Oregon, he had joined the U.S. Navy in August 2004. Immediately, his ship headed directly for Indonesia, arriving only twenty-four hours after the devastating wave struck. "The water was calm and eerie," recalled Armstrong in a personal interview with the author. What the navy personnel saw next was shocking. "There was livestock and garbage floating in the water. There were dead bodies everywhere."

Quickly, Armstrong and the other navy men and women set up a makeshift hospital to treat infections, mend wounds, and bind broken bones. Others worked fast to build an onboard system that created clean, safe drinking water. Rows and rows of 5-gallon (19-liter) jugs were filled up and loaded onto the ship's helicopters. Bags of rice and MREs, or prepared meals that are ready to eat, were loaded alongside and then flown to the hungry and thirsty Indonesians in need. "When we landed, they were so happy to see us," said Armstrong. "They came from everywhere." The USS *Abraham Lincoln* remained in the area for thirty days, treating the injured and providing food and water.

In January 2010, Armstrong was on his ship as it left San Diego and headed for Panama City. "That was when we heard about the earthquake in Haiti," he said. The ship went full power for a day and night to get to the demolished country. As soon as the navy crew members arrived, they

Naval personnel from the USS *Abraham Lincoln* work hard to get life-saving supplies to those struggling to cope with the aftermath of the tsunami in Banda Aceh, Sumatra, in Indonesia.

began transporting food and water to some of the smaller, outlying towns that had been cut off from supplies. "We used our small inflatable boats that were typically used for search and rescue to act as water taxis," stated Armstrong. The navy ship's crew stayed around for three weeks doing everything from treating the sick and delivering food and water to repairing generators and water pumps.

Although a scene like this one may sound like a key moment in a natural disaster movie, it is part of a true story and shows what working with the navy can be like. Helping others and making their lives a little better—especially in a time of great fear and loss—is a large part of what being in the navy means. No wonder its motto is "A Global Force for Good." Armstrong learned the meaning of the motto first-hand. "Before I joined the navy," he explained, "I thought it was all about war-oriented missions, but now I know that we all go to great lengths to help those less fortunate or in need. The navy is selfless, and it feels great to be part of something that helps and even saves people's lives."

The navy offers opportunities for many people to serve their country and help others, while also providing a career, giving an education, and allowing them to experience the world. Are you ready to find out more about life in the navy?

CHAPTER 1

EXPLORING REASONS, MAKING DECISIONS

H ave you ever thought about joining the armed forces when you're older? It is a huge decision. It is definitely not one that most people make easily. What is behind the idea?

The reasons people join the U.S. Navy, or any of the military branches, change from one person to the next. Although one person might want the comprehensive health care insurance for medical and dental coverage, many others are far more interested in finding out about the education they can obtain without cost to them through the navy. The U.S. Navy provides some of the most amazing training in a wide range of skills. Often, service in the navy can lead to some of the world's most exciting careers. It also offers job security. Unlike in the civilian world, in the navy, a person can't lose a job just because the economy is struggling. Walter Lee, petty officer third class, yeoman, is quoted on Navy.com as saying, "The Navy has paid 100 percent of my college tuition. My health care is covered. I receive food and housing allowances. . . . With benefits and security better than what I received as a civilian, I sleep very well at night." For information on what different navy positions' pay rates are, go to the Bureau of Labor Statistics at http://www.bls.gov/oco/ocos249.htm or the Military Pay Scale Chart at http://www.militaryfactory.com/military_pay_scale.asp.

Of course, excitement is a huge reason all by itself for enlisting! People often come in search of adventure and a chance to travel across the globe, seeing new countries and meeting all kinds of new people. "Since I've been in the navy . . . I have traveled to more than thirty-five countries in Europe, Asia, South America, the Middle East and all but six of the fifty states," says Travis Goodwin, supply corps officer, lieutenant commander on Navy.com. "Where else [would I be able to do that] but in the navy?"

"When I talk to juniors and seniors in high school," said Petty Officer Diane Underwood, a navy recruiter in Oregon, in a personal interview with the author, "I ask what do you know about the navy? They always answer, 'They have boats.' They often know little more than that." The navy generally appeals to some people because of where most of its action takes place: on the water! Whereas the air force often lures those who want to explore the sky, and the army and marines attract those who prefer

Standing on the bridge of an aircraft carrier to navigate the carrier across the ocean is one of the many exciting job opportunities in the navy.

land combat, the navy calls to those who love to spend time riding in all kinds of boats and swimming in every possible lake, river, or ocean.

What is life at sea really like? Most hours of the day are spent in whatever occupation the sailors and officers have chosen. However, there are free hours to fill as well. During these times, the men and women exercise, watch movies, play cards, write e-mails, or write letters to family and friends, eat, and even take extra classes.

How much time is actually spent at sea? That varies greatly from person to person. Most ships go to sea for ten to fourteen days every month for training operations. An extended mission can last as long as six months.

A primary reason many people give for joining the navy is a simple one: they want to defend and protect their country. A strong sense of patriotism, or devotion to their country, and a willingness to exchange a few years of their lives to support the United States are strong motivations for them. Many also want to change—to grow up—to become a strong adult, a goal that the navy can help them accomplish through a combination of time, education, and experience.

MEETING THE REQUIREMENTS

What does it take other than interest and willingness to become a navy sailor? The following are the initial basic requirements for enlistment (the voluntary enrollment in the military). You must be:

- Between the ages of eighteen and thirty-four. If you are seventeen years old, you must have parental consent.
- A U.S. citizen.
- A high school graduate, have a GED, or general equivalency diploma (a high school degree awarded after passing a series of examinations), or other high school equivalency requirements.

- Able to pass two urinalysis tests to prove you are alcohol and drug free.
- Free of any criminal history.

If a person is interested in pursuing training as an officer instead of an enlisted sailor, the navy has a slightly different set of requirements for that division. Besides having a high school diploma or GED, a person must be a college graduate with a four-year bachelor of science or bachelor of arts degree from an accredited university. These applicants must also have a high overall grade point average (GPA), but specific GPA requirements depend on the program of study.

MAKING THE SERVICE COMMITMENT

How long does a person typically serve in the navy if he or she signs on the dotted line? It depends on many factors. What education is the person hoping to receive? Does he or she want to be an enlisted sailor or an officer? Generally speaking, enlisted personnel's service ranges from two to four years, whereas officer positions range from three to five years.

So, how do people begin to make such a major decision? Typically, they start by talking to an expert—a navy recruiter. Recruiters have been specially trained to answer a wide array of questions and

Navy recruiters often visit high schools to answer students' questions and hand out helpful information to those considering a career in the armed services.

give people the exact information they need. One of the topics most recruiters will discuss is the different ways a person can enter the navy. These options include the following:

- Military Entrance Processing Station: A two-day test of a person's physical and academic abilities.
- Delayed Entry Program: An option to join without having to serve active duty immediately. This option gives people the time to take care of any

ONLINE SUPPORT

One way to learn more about the navy is through some Facebook sites. U.S. Navy Life (http://www.facebook.com/USNavyLife) has sailors who ask and answer all kinds of questions, from help for a single mom who wants to enlist to tips on getting through basic training. Women Redefined (http://www.facebook.com/womenredefinedNavy?v=info) is a site for women in the navy. It motto is "Applauding women who define life on their own terms. Intermingling the stereotypically feminine and masculine. Women in the Navy are amongst those paving the way in redefining femininity in the 21st century." For mothers of sons and daughters serving in the navy, there is support and encouragement at Navy for Moms, which states, "You gave them the values. We give them the oppor-tunity." It can be accessed at http://www.navyformoms.com. Twitter messages about the navy can be found at http://twitter.com/navynews.

personal matters, like quitting a job, moving, talk-ing to family, and so on.

- Undergraduate programs: this option allows the newly enlisted to join the navy and go to college simultaneously.
- Naval Reserve Officers Training Corps (NROTC): Students with high GPAs often choose this option, which gives them up to $180,000 in funds to cover tuition at 160 of the nation's top schools.

- Direct Appointment Program: This option is for college graduates or professionals who already have degrees. They are immediately made navy officers.

Most recruiters encourage young people to bring their parents to interviews as well. Having family and friends behind the decision to join the navy makes it easier for everyone involved. Bringing parents along gives them both the chance to ask their own questions and to feel better about what their sons or daughters are choosing to do with the next few years of their lives.

PUTTING IN AN APPLICATION

Filling out an application is best done with a recruiter nearby to answer questions. Before it can be completed, a candidate must provide a number of standard documents. For those applying to be an enlisted sailor, these include:

- Medical records
- Birth certificate
- Social Security card
- Citizenship certificate (if applicable)
- High school diploma
- Complete list of places you have been employed
- Four character references

10 QUESTIONS TO ASK A

NAVY RECRUITER

1. How long do I serve if I sign up?

2. What are the physical requirements to join the U.S. Navy?

3. What kinds of tests do I need to take to get in?

4. Do I need my parent's permission to enlist?

5. How do the perks and benefits compare to other military branches?

6. What is boot camp like?

7. Where will I be stationed?

8. What kinds of careers are open to me in the navy?

9. What else does the navy do other than water rescue?

10. How is the U.S. Navy different from the U.S. Coast Guard?

- List of any place you have visited outside of the United States
- List of all the places you have ever lived
- Any information pertaining to drug use or police involvement

For those who want to be officers, all of the above are needed, along with college transcripts and any medical or dental certifications and licenses that have been earned.

The application is in the works and now comes the hard part—being tested and then heading off to basic training, also known as boot camp. What will that be like? Is it as hard as it is portrayed in many movies? Maybe. For many people, it is a chance to find out just exactly what they are made of!

CHAPTER 2

GETTING READY, BEING TRAINED

Research the navy. Check. Talk to a recruiter. Check. Bring in the paperwork and fill out the application. Check. What's next? A two-day trip through the nearest Military Entrance Processing Station (MEPS).

First, a person has to take the Armed Services Vocational Aptitude Battery (ASVAB). This exam is designed to test a person's strengths and weaknesses. It helps an individual determine which careers fit him or her best. Instead of one test, it is a battery, or several tests put together. It contains two hundred questions and takes about three hours to complete.

The test starts with four basic eligibility tests. These are for making sure that applicants have basic academic knowledge. The questions are divided up into arithmetic reasoning, math knowledge, word knowledge, and paragraph comprehension. The next part of the test is specifically designed to see which

SOME SAMPLE ASVAB TEST QUESTIONS

The Web site Today's Military (http://www .todaysmilitary.com) describes the Armed Services Vocational Aptitude Battery (ASVAB) and its use in helping to identify the occupations that are best suited to the student's talents. The following questions are samples found on the Web site.

In Arithmetic Reasoning:

How many 36-passenger buses will it take to carry 144 people?

    A. 3
    B. 4
    C. 5
    D. 6

In Paragraph Comprehension:

Twenty-five percent of all household burglaries can be attributed to unlocked windows or doors. Crime is the result of opportunity plus desire. To prevent crime, it is each individual's responsibility to:

    A. provide the desire
    B. provide the opportunity
    C. prevent the desire
    D. prevent the opportunity

In Auto and Shop Information:

A car uses too much oil when which of the following parts are worn?
  A. pistons
  B. piston rings
  C. main bearings
  D. connecting rods

Answers: B, D, and B

(Source: http://www.todaysmilitary.com/before-serving-in-the-military/asvab-test/asvab-test-sample-questions)

military services the applicant might do best in. This part is separated into the subjects of Electronics Information, Mechanical Comprehension, Auto and Shop Information, and General Science. The minimum score required for the navy is thirty-five points.

LET'S GET PHYSICAL

Now that a person's academic abilities have been tested, it is time to check his or her physical condition. A physical examination, such as what people get from their doctors every year, is done. Recruiters want to make sure that incoming enlisted personnel do not have any serious health problems and will be able to complete the Navy Physical Readiness Test. The test consists of a 1.5 miles (2.4 kilometers) run, push-ups, and sit-ups. The navy tests blood and urine, does hearing and visual exams, documents height and weight, and checks overall physical flexibility. Men must be between 60 and 80 inches (between 1.5 and 2 meters) tall, and women should be between 58 and 80 inches (between 1.47 and 2 m) in height.

What medical conditions can disqualify a person? There are quite a few. Some have to do with health conditions, others with physical deformities or impairment of vision, hearing, or flexibility. A detailed list of medical disqualifications can be found at Military.com.

What else can possibly disqualify a person? If a person has a criminal record, it can be a problem. Sometimes a waiver can get the person in anyway, but it depends on the situation. The same is true for an individual with a history of any kind of substance (alcohol or drug) abuse.

If a person is not sure what field of study within the navy is most appealing, the Navy Life Ops quiz (http://www.navy.com/life-ops.html) can help him or her narrow it down. It explores a person's choices in activities and interests and then matches them up with potential careers. A career classifier can also help with choosing

The Navy Physical Readiness Test examines a person's ability to do all kinds of physical exercises, including curl-ups, which these sailors are performing.

the most appropriate job path. This counselor is specially trained in matching your interest, your test results, and your physical abilities with just the right jobs.

Once the enlistment contract has been signed, it is time to celebrate! People usually invite their parents, brothers and sisters, and friends to the Oath of Enlistment Ceremony. At the gathering, a person raises his or her right hand and states:

I, _____, do solemnly swear (or affirm) that I will support and defend the Constitution of the United States against all enemies, foreign and domestic; that I will bear true faith and allegiance to the same; and that I will obey the orders of the President of the United States and the orders of the officers appointed over me, according to regulations and the Uniform Code of Military Justice. So help me God.

It's official! The person is now in the navy. Each branch of the military also tends to have its own creed that it recites. For the navy, it is the Sailor's Creed, as follows:

I am a United States Sailor.
I will support and defend the Constitution of the United States of America and I will obey the orders of those appointed over me.

Taking the official Oath of Enlistment is an exciting moment for all future sailors—their hard work and determination have paid off and adventure is waiting just ahead.

I represent the fighting spirit of the Navy and those who have gone before me to defend freedom and democracy around the world.
I proudly serve my country's Navy combat team with Honor, Courage and Commitment.
I am committed to excellence and the fair treatment of all.

THE EXPERIENCE OF BOOT CAMP

Various stories of Recruit Basic Training, or boot camp, can be found in books, movies, and television shows. To most people, boot camp looks loud, painful, and challenging. In some ways, these descriptions are true. Boot camp is designed to help regular men and women turn into military personnel. In the navy, boot camp lasts for eight weeks. Drill instructors teach new recruits how to function as a team. They also train them in the following areas:

- First aid
- Water survival skills
- Marksmanship
- Tactics
- Customs, traditions, and history of the navy

During the first week, recruits are given navy-issued clothes, dental and medical exams, and, most likely, haircuts. They will be instructed on exactly how their belongings are to be stored and how their beds are to be made. Most waking hours will be filled with a mixture of classes and physical training, including swimming, marching, and drilling. The second week concentrates on building each person's confidence. Everyone is taught what to do in a shipboard emergency, learning that each person's

THE DARKER SIDE

Although joining the navy may be the perfect choice for someone—sometimes it is not. Life in the military is not right for everyone. Enlisting means promising to give several years of one's life over to the complete control of others. It means doing what a person is told, no questions asked, from what time to get up in the morning to what to eat, wear, and do 24/7.

Here are a few questions each person should give a great deal of thought to before joining any military branch:

1. What are my real reasons for wanting to join? (If it is to get out of jail time or recover from a broken heart or just get away from family and/or your hometown, these are not good reasons.)

2. How do I feel about taking and following orders? (Can you do what you're told without asking questions or protesting? Can you do it every single day?)

3. Am I willing to do a great deal of physical exercise? Am I capable of it? (Boot camp is tough and so are many missions. Are you up to the physical demands?)

4. Can I handle being miles away from my family and friends for months to years at a time? (For some, this is a real perk—for others, homesickness can be unbearable.)

(CONTINUED ON PAGE 26)

THE DARKER SIDE (CONTINUED)

5. Can I accept that, even if I don't like it or it is nothing like I had imagined, quitting isn't really an option? (Getting out of the military once a person is in it is very difficult.)

6. Am I willing to be injured or even give up my life for this? (Although you may never see face-to-face combat or be in a war situation, you have to be willing to do so at any time.)

survival depends on the rest of the team following through as well.

Week three of boot camp is a "hands-on" week. It will be spent mostly on a training ship that is secured on land. Recruits are taught proper names of all parts of the ship and how to send signals with flags, a communication method known as semaphore. Classes will emphasize how to communicate on board ship, how to identify the different classifica-tions of navy ships and aircraft, and the laws of basic seamanship. The first physical test is held dur-ing this third week. During week four, recruits get to handle weapons for the first time, learning how to use an M-16 rifle and a 12-gauge shotgun. Practice will be held at a live fire range. The fourth week also includes an academic test of what has been learned by the recruit to date.

Week five focuses on making career choices. Recruits explore possible jobs within the navy and set their goals. Week six ramps up the action, as the emphasis is on firefighting training. Knowing what to do to control fire damage on board a ship is one of the most important skills anyone in the navy learns. Some of the abilities learned during the sixth week include how to do the following:

- Extinguish fires
- Escape smoke-filled compartments
- Open and close watertight doors
- Operate an oxygen breathing apparatus
- Carry fire hoses

During the sixth week, recruits also have to pass the challenging Confidence Chamber test. About one hundred recruits are put into a large chamber and everyone puts on a gas mask. A tear gas tablet is lit and each person has to take off his or her mask and recite his or her full name and Social Security number. They cannot exit until the entire row finishes. Usually, they come out gagging, spitting, and vomiting—but they survive.

In week seven of boot camp, the navy puts the recruits to the ultimate test with Battle Stations.

Donning a gas mask and walking into the Confidence Chamber, where recruits experience mild tear gas, is never easy and takes courage. The pride of having built up confidence in the use of a gas mask (and trusting that it will work in a contaminated environment), though, makes the experience worthwhile.

Everyone is faced with a dozen different scenarios that test everything that has been taught since week one. Teams must work together and are graded as a whole on how well everyone performed their individual roles. Once finished, recruits are handed the prize—the U.S. Navy ball cap. It is a symbol to everyone that recruit days are over. They are navy sailors now!

Week eight of boot camp is the best of all—graduation. New sailors put on their uniforms, family and friends come, and each recruit is now officially a sailor in the U.S. Navy!

After boot camp ends, what comes next? Most of the enlisted personnel will head off to "A School." This school is where they receive their technical training. As the weeks pass, the sailors are allowed more and more freedom, especially compared to boot camp. While the enlisted are in A School, officers head to either Officer Candidate School or Officer Development School.

Officer Candidate School is located at the Naval Station Newport in Rhode Island. It lasts for twelve weeks and is designed to train college graduates to become officers. Classes center on leadership, physical and military training, and academics. Officer Development School is taught at the same location but only lasts for five weeks. It is tailored for already commissioned officers who are pursuing a specific course of study.

After school, sailors sometimes get a few days to visit home before they are sent to their first duty station. Petty Officer Diane Underwood remembers that moment very well. "I left my hometown in Illinois right after Christmas. The wind chill was 80 degrees below zero [-62 degrees Celsius] at the airport and I was all bundled up. My duty station was in Hawaii. I had never been beyond the Midwest," she explained in a personal interview with the author. "I arrived in the Hawaii airport dressed in my navy blues and it was 88°F (31°C), hot and humid! I was eighteen years old and I looked out at Diamond Head and all I could think was, 'You are on your own for the first time in the middle of paradise.'"

To help new sailors get used to the area they have been sent to, the navy sends a packet of information months ahead of time with helpful information. It includes details about the job market (for spouses), housing, and more. Each person is also given a navy sponsor to help with the transition. "Your sponsor is your mentor," said Underwood. "He or she introduces you around, helps you to get settled and is there to help create a road map of your goals, plus give you support when life happens."

Where do new recruits live? It depends on where they are stationed. If they begin on a base, they typically live in barracks, although families sometimes are situated in apartments or houses located on or near the base. The quarters usually are unfurnished, other than a few basic appliances. The utilities are taken care of by the housing allowance and many homes have three to four bedrooms, with homey touches such as porches and yards.

Those recruits that are immediately stationed on a ship or submarine at sea, on the other hand, are given a "berthing area." This includes a locker for storing clothing and a few belongings and a "rack" or bed

The berthing area on this guided-missile frigate, a type of warship, is small and tight and requires sailors to keep their belongings to a minimum. Privacy is maintained through a simple curtain that can be opened and closed.

for sleeping. Free time is often spent in the "mess decks" or kitchen areas where everyone can eat, watch television, play games, and write letters to family and friends.

The journey from wondering what it would be like to be in the navy to putting on the uniform and choosing a career path is a long and challenging one. Once it has been made, however, a world of opportunities opens up for sailors, as there is a position for everyone.

CHAPTER 3

CAREERS IN ARTS AND EDUCATION

How in the world does a career in arts and education fit in with the navy? Surprisingly, it fits quite well. Photographers take amazing shots of people and places in the countries they visit. Musicians play for important national and international government events. Chaplains counsel homesick sailors, and translators make it possible to communicate with those from other cultures. The possible pathways for this career include arts and photography, religion, education, music, news and media, and world languages. What skills are the most helpful to possess if you choose one of these routes?

ARTS AND PHOTOGRAPHY

Do you love to capture candid shots of people? Are you eager to grab a shot of a statue, building, or historic site? Do you pay close attention to the angle of the light and shadows? Perhaps you would prefer to

Capturing the memories and documenting the places you travel, the people you meet, and the events you witness are essential duties within the navy's arts and education career field.

write about these people, places, and events? If so, becoming a navy mass communication specialist (MC) could be a perfect choice for you. You can channel those artistic talents and use them as a way to connect and communicate with not only the navy but also the public. You might take pictures of global disasters or create multimedia profiles of important officers. You can design elaborate Web sites or write an important press announcement. Your words and images might be seen locally, nationally, and even internationally.

In this role as a public affairs and visual information expert, you can expect to do the following:

- Record and edit regular photography, as well as digital video, of military operations and exercises, along with other navy events
- Write, edit, and produce articles about news events for use in military and civilian newspapers and magazines, as well as television and radio broadcast stories
- Create graphic designs to be used on official Web sites
- Serve as a navy professional photographer
- Learn how to operate and use state-of-the-art photography and video equipment
- Accompany the troops out in the field, acting as a combat cameraman
- Take photos of important events for both publication and for documentation of what occurred
- Help the public affairs officers before any media briefings
- Work closely with radio and television stations to deliver news and other announcements

A NAVY PHOTOGRAPHER

Over the years, many navy sailors and officers have gone on to different kinds of fame. Six former U.S. presidents were in the navy, including Jimmy Carter, Richard Nixon, Gerald Ford, Lyndon B. Johnson, John F. Kennedy, and George H. W. Bush. In September 1943, after Bush finished his training in flight, he was assigned to be the photographer for his torpedo squadron.

War veteran and renowned photographer Edward J. Steichen (1879–1973) once told navy photographers that they should not photograph the war, but the people who fought it. In other words, photographing a seaman enables photographers to capture the heartache and dreams of an individual. With a job in arts and education, that is exactly what many sailors are able to do.

EDUCATION

From the day you walked into boot camp, you've been learning nonstop. You've learned countless skills, and now, with this career path, you have the chance to share everything with others. You might find yourself lecturing to a classroom or deep inside a navy ship giving a hands-on lesson about engines. You

Sharing your knowledge and skills with others by teaching is another option in the navy's arts and education career area. Many lessons are hands-on, like this training class on repairing small boat outboard engines.

might teach in small groups or at huge conferences. Specific responsibilities in education will include providing the following:

- Hands-on classroom or group training
- Facts, details, advice, and help on a wide variety of topics
- Instruction to fellow personnel on different navy policies, procedures, and safety requirements
- Assistance in recruiting and career counseling

Many people who have entered the teaching profession have said that one of the best ways to learn information well is to turn around and teach it. As a navy educator, you get the chance to learn, share, and help others reach their goals.

MUSIC

Can singing or playing an instrument be part of being in the navy? It sure can. If you pursue a specialization in music, you might find yourself singing in the White House or playing piano in the Pentagon. You could be performing for foreign dignitaries or representing the navy on television or in a parade. You may be part of the U.S. Navy Band in Washington, D.C., the band at the U.S. Naval Academy in Annapolis, Maryland, or one of the numerous Navy Fleet bands. For training, you will be sent to the Armed Forces School of Music in Little Creek, Virginia.

Specific responsibilities that go with this position include:

- Performing a wide variety of music styles from jazz, rock, and soul to pop, country, and Broadway songs
- Participating in marching, concert, stage, and dance bands
- Conducting, rehearsing, and performing alone or in a group for radio and television broadcasts

- Writing and arranging music for events and performances
- Giving concerts for military ceremonies, parades, and other gatherings
- Performing for navy personnel, for the general public, and for diplomatic events

You may never have realized that composing songs, being able to play anything you hear, or simply having an ability to hit the right notes every time could lead to a career in the navy, but it is indeed possible. Chances are you will perform in front of some of the most impressive audiences in the world, too.

NEWS AND MEDIA

Can you stay calm in chaos? Can you operate as the eyes and the ears of the entire fleet on behalf of the rest of the world? If you think you can handle these responsibilities, you might want to pursue a career in news and media. This job is all about providing video, audio, and written materials to the national and international public. You may share this information through online sites or radio stations. You might write for the newspaper or television. This job requires meeting deadlines and communicating extremely clearly.

Some of the specific responsibilities of the job include:

News and media professionals draft public service announcements and other materials for naval personnel, including admirals, to present to daily news programs.

- Gathering facts for writing speeches and articles
- Writing, editing, proofreading, and producing radio and TV news, programs, and training films
- Preparing layouts for newspapers, magazines, and Web sites
- Operating as a staff photographer
- Scanning and editing digital video images, as well as digital editing
- Operating all kinds of state-of-the-art still and video equipment

Journalists are commonly right where the action is, and this is certainly true for anyone who follows the news or media career path in the navy. You will not only get the chance to use some of the most complex and sophisticated equipment in the field, but you will also keep the country connected to what is happening in all parts of the world.

WORLD LANGUAGES

Are you quick to pick up other languages? Understanding foreign languages is a skill that is needed constantly in the armed services. Being able to translate various languages makes it possible for different cultures to understand one another, and communication is the key to peace. You might be helping two dignitaries to understand each other or translating top-secret materials. A deep understanding of a language, including slang, idioms, and gestures, can make a real difference in a mission.

Notable tasks for this job include the following:

- Operating state-of-the-art electronic radio receivers, magnetic recording devices, computers, and communications signals equipment
- Listening to/reading classified information
- Translating and interpreting foreign language communications
- Analyzing and reporting foreign technical data or strategic and/or tactical information to fleet commanders and other superiors

THE U.S. NAVY ATHLETES

Staying in excellent physical shape is an essential part of having a life in the navy. How essential it is depends largely on which section of the navy you are part of. The minimum fitness qualification requirements are as follows:

Event	General Navy	SEAL	Special Warfare Combatant Craft Crewman	Navy Diver and Aviation Rescue Swimmer	Explosive Ordnance Disposal Technician
Push-Ups	46	42	42	42	42
Sit-Ups	54	50	50	50	50
Pull-Ups	NA	6	6	4	6
1.5-Mile (2.4 km) Run	12:15	11:00	12:30	12:00	12:45
500-Yard (457 m) Swim	12:15	12:30	13:00	12:00	14:00

- Performing temporary duty aboard different naval surface and subsurface vessels and aircraft

The career fields in arts and education give many people the chance to develop their biggest passions for words and images in a way that helps, supports, and expands the U.S. Navy. Where could it take you?

CAREERS IN AVIATION

A viation? How does that fit into a military branch that focuses on being out on the water? To the surprise of many, flight is an important element of the U.S. Navy. A career in aviation will lead you to piloting some of the most technologically advanced aircraft in existence. You might find yourself handling the complicated communications going to and from the plane or perfecting navigation techniques. Perhaps you will be in charge of updating and maintaining the aircraft's weapon systems. It is an exciting and constantly changing field!

NAVAL AVIATORS

Being a navy pilot or naval flight officer (NFO) may mean that from the air you are chasing an enemy submarine or searching for underwater mines. It may mean flying up higher than you can imagine or just

Being part of the navy's aviation program does not necessarily mean being a pilot. You might also find yourself guiding the pilots through preflight checks aboard an aircraft carrier to ensure a safe takeoff.

LCDR P. J. TILL

04

skimming above the surface of the sea. This position requires a four-year college degree. Pilots and NFOs fly some of the most high-tech aircraft ever invented, while they provide the attack, defense, and logistic support the sailors require.

Navy pilots and NFOs fly a wide variety of aircraft. There are thousands to choose from. Today, it might be an F/A-18 Super Hornet Jet and the next day an SH-60 Seahawk helicopter. After attending Officer Candidate School, you attend a six-week course at Naval Aviation Schools Command in Pensacola, Florida, and then onto primary flight training, followed by advanced training.

A pilot's specific responsibilities include learning about the following:

- Submarine warfare
- Mine countermeasures
- Search and rescue operations
- Advanced tactical systems
- Enemy surveillance through the collection of photographic intelligence

A NFO's particular duties include studies in these areas:

- Aerodynamics
- Aircraft engine systems

- Meteorology
- Navigation
- Flight planning
- Flight safety
- Specialization in EA-6B Prowler electronic counter-measures aircraft, F/A-18 Hornet and Super Hornet jet fighters, E-2C Hawkeye early warning and control aircraft, and P-3C antisubmarine aircraft
- Electronic detection of ships, submarines, aircraft, and missiles

NFOs are an essential part of the navy. Although the navy's presence is on the water, it needs eyes in the sky as well.

FLIGHT OPERATIONS

If you can imagine standing on an aircraft carrier's flight deck and guiding an aircraft into a safe landing or running a computer-based ground-controlled navigation and radar approach system, then flight operations might be a great vocation for you.

The two positions under this heading are navy aircrewman and air traffic controller. They carry out many of the jobs below and above the actual flight deck, making sure that every pilot and NFO takes off and lands safely. No college degree is required for these two occupations.

The abilities to multitask and stay alert are put to the test for those who choose to become air traffic controllers in the navy. Keeping a close eye on all flight operations is a challenging, but exhilarating, career choice.

Some of the duties for these positions involve the following:

- Performing aircraft technical duties as a flight engineer, loadmaster (who supervises the loading, rigging, and weight of cargo), and/or reel operator (who controls and uses the in-flight wire antenna systems)
- Handling duties related to launching and recovering naval aircraft
- Interpreting data on radar screens to plot aircraft positions
- Operating tactical weapons, sensors, and communication equipment

MEET THE X-47B

Fascinated by flight but not sure you want to be the one steering? In February 2011, the navy tested a new aircraft called the X-47B. It looks like a small B-2 Stealth bomber, and it flew at 5,000 feet (1,524 m) for almost half an hour. It was a successful first flight—but it did not have one important thing: a pilot. "Today we got a glimpse towards the future as the navy's first-ever tailless, jet-powered unmanned aircraft took to the skies," reports Captain Jaime Engdahwl, program manager for the Unmanned Combat Air System Demonstration, according to the *International Business Times*. Rear Admiral Bill Shannon adds, "We are breaking new ground by developing the first unmanned jet aircraft to take off and land aboard a flight deck."

- Working with pilots to operate and control aircraft systems
- Performing preflight planning, equipment checks, and postflight maintenance
- Maintaining aeronautical charts and maps
- Managing advanced airborne electronic equipment
- Acting as a flight communications operator

From pilot to air traffic controller, navigator to flight engineer, there are quite a few ways to be part of the aerial navy.

FLIGHT SUPPORT

Pilots, NFOs, and other flight personnel could not possibly do their jobs without those in flight support. These sailors are the ones that maintain the aircraft, inspecting engines and propellers to make sure they are in good shape. They also provide essential attack, defense, and logistic support to the rest of the fleet.

Becoming a navy flight support team member does not require a college degree. The person in this position is responsible for operating and maintaining hydraulic and steam catapults to launch the aircraft, and running and sustaining landing gear, brakes, and related systems.

Navy aviation maintenance duty officers, on the other hand, do require a college degree. Their responsibilities encompass the following:

- Overseeing that all aircraft maintenance has been performed correctly
- Understanding newly designed aviation weapon systems so that repairs and maintenance are kept to a minimum
- Providing operational support to the fleet's personnel and aircraft
- Managing all material and manpower needed to support flight operations

AVIATION RESCUE SWIMMERS

Considering what aviation rescue swimmers do on a regular basis, it comes as little surprise that their motto is "So Others May Live." These specially trained men and women are the people who plunge into cold water to save crew members in trouble. They carefully slide down a rope from a hovering helicopter to reach survivors at crash sites or in the middle of hurricanes.

Rescue swimmers are part of the world's best emergency response teams that save lives. The job takes not only a great amount of skill and strength but also bravery, as very few missions are without danger. Many of them involve jumping out of helicopters into the chilly, churning sea below.

The training for this position is long and intense, usually taking about two years to complete. It includes courses in water and land survival; flight safety; search and rescue swimming skills; survival, evasion, resistance, and escape (SERE) techniques; and aircraft systems. Some aviation rescue swimmers choose to get additional training in emergency medicine or attend Advanced Rescue Swimmer School, which encompasses instruction in swift water, high seas, and cave and cliff rescue.

After graduation, rescue swimmers may be assigned to a helicopter combat squadron, helicopter antisubmarine squadron, a helicopter antisubmarine squadron light, or a helicopter maritime strike squadron at sea or on shore.

(CONTINUED ON PAGE 50)

AVIATION RESCUE SWIMMERS (CONTINUED)

Some of the duties called for in being a rescue swimmer include:

- Saving pilots from crashed or nonfunctioning aircraft, people on stranded or sinking boats, and even hikers/mountain climbers in danger on land
- Rescuing civilians during a variety of natural disasters
- Working on helicopters to make sure rescue swimmers and pilots are communicating and operating the hoist as a team
- Delivering aid and supplies to other countries in need
- Providing support to Naval Special Warfare Operations
- Transporting troops and cargo to and from ships
- Conducting surveillance in antisubmarine warfare and drug interdiction operations

If you are a strong swimmer and enjoy the rush of adrenaline that comes from helping people in danger, being a rescue swimmer could be the perfect choice for you. The job takes equal parts strength, bravery, and determination!

Although the navy tends to focus on ships, its air support is a vital part of its fleet. The contributions of the men and women who work in these aviation fields are in large part why the navy remains a strong global force for good.

CHAPTER 5

CAREERS IN BUSINESS AND LAW

Do business people and attorneys have a place within the navy? They certainly do. If you have a talent for accounting, law, or management, this is the career area for you to explore.

FINANCE AND ACCOUNTING

Can you imagine being put in charge of a payroll worth $2 million—every two weeks? If you are in accounting, you could be. That amount is the average two-week payroll on a navy aircraft carrier. It is your job to make sure everyone gets a paycheck for the right amount and on time. In this division, you might also be put in charge of inventory—a tricky job of making sure there are always enough supplies in the ship's stores. Sometimes you might even find yourself repairing and stocking vending machines and automatic teller machines (ATMs).

Some of the specific responsibilities that a position in accounting and finance includes are:

Mail is an important lifeline for all navy personnel, so post offices are happy places to work. Whether distributing letters in the onboard post office, keeping track of the ship's inventory, or portioning the payroll, the people in finance and accounting provide smooth operations for a ship's crew or on base.

- Creating regular payroll
- Recording and controlling travel expense payments
- Making cash sales and transactions
- Providing regular maintenance of the ship's ATMs
- Opening and running navy post offices
- Handling registered, certified, and special classes of mail in a secure manner
- Maintaining and ordering necessary supplies
- Keeping close inventory on the various items in the ships' stores
- Updating and maintaining all inventory records

Working in this field involves all elements of small business management, retail and marketing, accounting, and customer service.

BUSINESS MANAGEMENT

Sailors cannot do their jobs if they don't have the right materials and equipment to use; therefore, management becomes quite essential. People in business management tally the columns, create spreadsheets, and juggle numbers at sea and on shore.

A job in naval business management includes using basic computer knowledge plus software to keep and record information, understanding fundamental principles of retail and marketing, knowing how to both develop and implement various business strategies, and being able to solve complicated problems and make solid decisions. All these responsibilities require excellent oral and written skills.

A job in naval business management includes these responsibilities:

- Preparing inventory records and correspondence
- Ordering, receiving, and issuing spare parts, clothing, and general supplies
- Managing and operating retail and service activities ashore, afloat, or on a sub
- Using computers to track and maintain inventory and to track shipboard retail and service activities

- Operating office equipment and cash registers
- Keeping accounting records

If multitasking is easy for you and you can keep track of several lists in your head at once, business management could be a perfect fit. You will have many chances to organize and keep the navy in order.

PURCHASING, SUPPLY, AND LOGISTICS

The people who work in this field truly are the life-blood of the fleet because they make sure that supplies, materials, and equipment get where they need to go, when they need to be there. The navy has to be ready at all times to go wherever it is needed, and to do that, it depends largely on people in purchasing, supply, and logistics. If you're exceptional at math and can juggle numbers without losing track, and if you're highly organized, this occupation may be a perfect fit.

Supply corps positions require a college degree. This career area encompasses the following tasks:

- Analyzing the need for supplies and predicting future needs
- Managing the inspection, shipping, handling, and packaging of supplies and equipment

- Directing personnel who receive inventory and issue supplies and equipment
- Evaluating bids and proposals submitted by potential suppliers
- Studying ways to use space and distributing supplies efficiently
- Determining the fastest and most economical way to transport cargo or personnel
- Overseeing the handling of special items (medicines, explosives, etc.)

Clearly, this position has more authority and puts you in charge of making sure that others do what is needed to keep the navy supplied and ready to go.

The purchasing and supply position does not require a degree. The job responsibilities entail the following:

- Keeping financial records
- Ordering, storing, checking, and issuing naval aircraft and aeronautical equipment and accessories
- Preparing inventory reports and correspondence
- Keeping official publications up-to-date
- Maintaining financial logs
- Operating computer systems that help monitor submarine supplies and performing accounting functions
- Organizing and operating navy post offices, both on land and at sea

DAY AT THE NAVEL ACADEMY

What is life inside the Naval Academy in Annapolis, Maryland, like? Each day is structured tightly to get everything covered. A typical day looks like this:

TIME	EVENT
5:30 AM	Arise for personal fitness workout
6:30	All hands out of bed/reveille
6:30–7:00	Special instruction period for plebes
7:00	Morning meal formation
7:10	Breakfast
7:55-11:45	Four class periods of one hour each
12:05 PM	Noon meal formation
12:15	Noon meal
12:40–1:20	Company training time
1:30–3:30	Fifth and sixth class periods
3:30–6:00	Athletics, extracurricular and personal activities, drill and parades in fall and spring
5:00–7:00	Supper
7:30–11:00	Study period
11:00	Lights out

Of course, there are a few minutes here and there for some fun. The list of extracurricular activities is a long one but includes everything from Glee Club and Pipes and Drums to Chess Club, Rock Climbing Club, and Oceanography Club.

Enjoying paperwork, keeping lists, working with numbers, and anticipating people's needs are all skills that fall into this category of naval jobs. If you feel that these are your strengths, the perfect career fit may just be within this department.

ATTORNEY AND LEGAL SUPPORT

Do you want to help sailors create wills? Are you interested in helping negotiate international agreements? A legal career might be a wise choice, then. There are two distinct pathways in this field. One is open to enlisted personnel who do not have a degree. The other is available to those who have graduated from law school or are within two years of graduation.

The first position is known as a legalman. A legalman's duties can involve the following:

- Providing assistance to sailors and their families
- Serving as office managers
- Assisting in preparation of legal forms, letters, and requests
- Maintaining records and official publications
- Preparing official accounts of hearings, investigations, courts martial, and courts of inquiry
- Processing appeals

Being a judge advocate general in the navy may mean making visits to foreign countries, such as Iraq, to talk to navy attorneys and paralegals and to oversee trials and review court cases.

In many ways, this position is similar to a paralegal in the civilian world. It gives you a chance to be a part of the law without obtaining a degree first.

The other position, which requires a law degree, is within the Judge Advocate General's Corps (JAG). Those within JAG provide legal expertise for all aspects of the law. If you would like to pursue a position in this division, you would be working in these areas:

- Military justice
- Legal assistance
- International law
- Operational law
- Administrative law
- Environmental law
- Civil litigation
- Humanitarian assistance
- Refugee law
- Admiralty and maritime law

This position in the navy has intrigued many people, partly because of a long running television series called *JAG*, which was broadcast from 1995 to 2005. Being a naval lawyer may just be what you've wanted the most.

HUMAN RESOURCES

Perhaps you are a "people person"? Do you enjoy listening and talking to people and finding ways to help them? If so, human resources is one of the best career areas for you to choose. You will be the person who has the answers to everyone's questions and knows all there is to know about navy procedures, occupations, educational opportunities, job training, and wages. Individuals in this position are an important link between people and management.

The major functions within this type of job include:

- Providing counseling related to navy positions, job training, promotions, rights, and benefits
- Interviewing personnel for assignment recommendations
- Assisting the enlisted and their families with any particular problems or personal issues
- Establishing and maintaining a liaison with the Navy Personnel Command
- Providing counseling and career guidance
- Managing a duty station's Career Information Program

Remember the sign-up procedure and the career counselor you could meet at that time? If the type of work that this position requires appeals to you, this might be the division for you to explore further.

OFFICE AND ADMINISTRATIVE SUPPORT

Another option for those who excel in the skills of managing and organizing is the office and administrative support career path. It is often described as the "heart" of navy operations. An administrator position does not require a college degree.

With this type of job, you will excel at these duties:

- Providing individual guidance and counseling about rights and benefits, career path options, promotion requirements, and educational opportunities
- Supporting chaplains of all faiths, so as to provide religious support or advice on personal hardships and family matters, operating and managing religious ministry facilities on shore or at sea, and assisting in the preparation of devotional and religious educational materials
- Interviewing personnel and administering tests

Dealing with piles of paper is a part of every organization, including the navy. If you like to read, scan, file, organize, and juggle words on paper, there is probably a position that perfectly suits you.

- Preparing subpoenas and powers of attorney, processing appeals, investigating claims, scheduling courtrooms, and notifying people involved
- Scheduling and issuing aircraft inspections and work orders and maintaining aircraft and engine logbooks and associated records
- Operating personal computers, word processors, duplicate machines, audio recording devices, and other office machines
- Maintaining personnel, legal, and administrative records, writing official letters, reports, and correspondence, and providing clerical assistance

In most of these jobs, you will become a person who can perform many different types of work. You will know a great deal about various divisions and be the person others seek out when they have a question, problem, or dilemma.

PUBLIC AFFAIRS

The public affairs office is for the "people person" who has extraordinary skills. This position is all about people and the media in all of its aspects. Job tasks could be as small as a newspaper interview or as large as a presidential visit. You could be writing a speech for an admiral one week and giving a lecture to a high school class the next. People in this job are

RULES FOR WOMEN

Are women welcome in the navy? Absolutely! Currently, there are more than fifty-two thousand women on active duty. In an Armed Services Press Service report, Navy Secretary Ray Mabus stated, "We literally could not run the navy without women today." When women enlist, they undergo the same training as men do. They are given separate living quarters, of course. Women are also expected to have the same standards of appearance as men, except that they can wear their hair somewhat longer. Women are free to apply for and hold any job in the U.S. Navy with a single exception. They are not allowed to join the Navy SEALs.

Until recently, women were not allowed to serve on submarines, but by 2012, that rule will change. Congress decided in May 2010 that female officers can be assigned to submarines after all. Although there are some concerns that a coed crew will lead to sexual misconduct, Rear Admiral and top submarine commander Barry Bruner stated to reporter Russ Bynum, "We're going to look back on this four or five years from now, shrug our shoulders and say, 'What was everybody worrying about?'"

the link that connects the news and the public. You deal with visual, audio, and written communications. This career area requires a college degree.

In this position, you will find yourself:

- Supervising the writing and delivery of press releases and reports, and providing information to news media and various organizations
- Briefing military personnel before they meet with the public and news media, and scheduling and conducting news conferences
- Overseeing the content and production of radio and television programs, newspapers, magazines, and Web sites
- Advising the operational commander about decision making and communication with the media, internal navy, and the public

In many ways, the person in this role becomes the face of the navy. It is a huge responsibility but also one of the most exciting career areas. If being in the spotlight feels good to you, explore this field first!

CHAPTER 6

CAREERS IN KEEPING THE BODY AND SOUL HEALTHY

Is faith an important part of your life? For many of the men and women enlisted in the navy, it is. Just because they are off serving their country, it does not mean that they ignore their religious beliefs. Instead, these beliefs often become deeper and more important. If faith, regardless of a particular religion, is a high priority to you, consider becoming a chaplain or religious program specialist. Remember that you must be tolerant of all religious faiths—and respect them.

CHAPLAINS

The navy has more than eight hundred chaplains in it, covering more than one hundred different kinds of faith, including Protestant, Catholic, Jewish, Muslim, and Buddhist. These men and women talk to sailors and pray with them, counsel them, advise them, and help them. Their job is to support and care for all

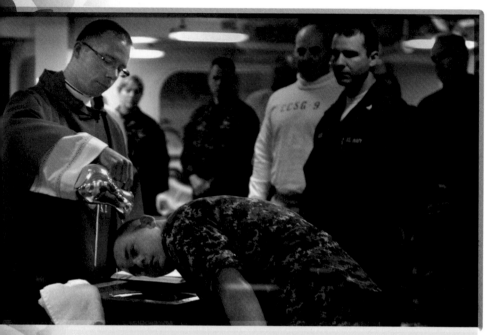

One part of a navy chaplain's job might be baptizing sailors while on board a ship. Meeting the spiritual needs of the crew is a vital part of every mission.

service members and their families and protect each person's right to freedom of religion. Sometimes it means helping people through some of their most challenging and painful moments, while at other times, it means celebrating and rejoicing together.

This job requires a college degree. The specific responsibilities of this position include the following:

- Conducting worship services in different settings
- Performing religious rites and ceremonies such as weddings, funerals, and baptisms

- Counseling those looking for guidance
- Overseeing religious education programs (Sunday school, youth groups, etc.)
- Providing spiritual guidance and care to hospitalized personnel and/or family members
- Training others to conduct religious education programs
- Promoting attendance at religious services and other events
- Advising leaders regarding the issues of morale, ethics, and spiritual well-being

Chaplain Michael Mueller wrote about the job on the U.S. Navy's Web site, saying,

Each navy chaplain is motivated by his or her own sense of calling. For me, it wasn't thunderbolts or lightning, but a gradual process. Over the years in my civilian ministry, I saw a lot of band-aid ministry—but it was difficult to effect any real change in people's lives.
In the navy, that all changes. Sailors and marines are looking for real guidance, searching for that higher sense of spirituality. They're ready for their souls to be truly touched.
Navy chaplains are surgeons of the soul—even more so than a civilian minister. And the potential to save lives is immeasurable.

RELIGIOUS PROGRAM SPECIALIST

A religious program specialist (RPS) is an important assistant to the chaplains. This position does not require a college degree. As an RPS, you will do everything you can to support the chaplain's programs and projects. The role goes beyond an administrative one, though. Chaplains are not allowed to carry any weapons. As a religious program specialist, you are in charge of protecting the chaplain wherever he or she might travel.

Some of the duties required for this job are as follows:

- Supporting clergy of all faiths in religious activities
- Providing physical security for chaplains during field exercise and in combat environments
- Maintaining records, documents, and references for various faith groups
- Operating, managing, and maintaining religious ministry facilities on land and at sea
- Assisting in the preparation of devotional and religious educational materials and audiovisual displays
- Handling all phases of the support needed for religious programs on ships, on shore, and in hospitals
- Operating and maintaining libraries
- Publicizing the command's religious activities

To find out more about the U.S. Navy Chaplain Corps, check it out on Facebook at http://www .facebook.com/navychaplain?v=info.

HEALTH CARE

Not surprisingly, one of the biggest divisions in the navy is the health care department. In fact, the navy has more than 4,300 physicians, 1,200 dentists, 3,900 nurses, and 2,600 administrative, research, and clinical specialists. Have you dreamed of being part of the medical services profession? This career area may be a perfect fit for you. You may find yourself providing first aid to survivors at a crash site, helping fellow sailors recover from an injury, or tending to the families of sailors when they are ill. You will work in one of more than 250 medical facilities on shore, at sea, and within the field, often using state-of-the-art equipment and techniques. These health care professionals also serve on one of the two dedicated hospital ships, the USNS *Comfort* and the USNS *Mercy*.

MEDICAL CORPS

Being a physician in the medical corps is a huge responsibility. There are more than thirty specialty areas you could pursue. They cover a broad range from dermatology and neurology to obstetrics and surgery. You attend medical school through the navy. Specific responsibilities encompass the following:

Medical personnel on board navy ships, including the USNS *Comfort*, do more than take care of their own. They often examine and treat those wounded in natural disasters, such as Haiti's 2010 devastating earthquake and Japan's 2011 earthquakes and catastrophic tsunami.

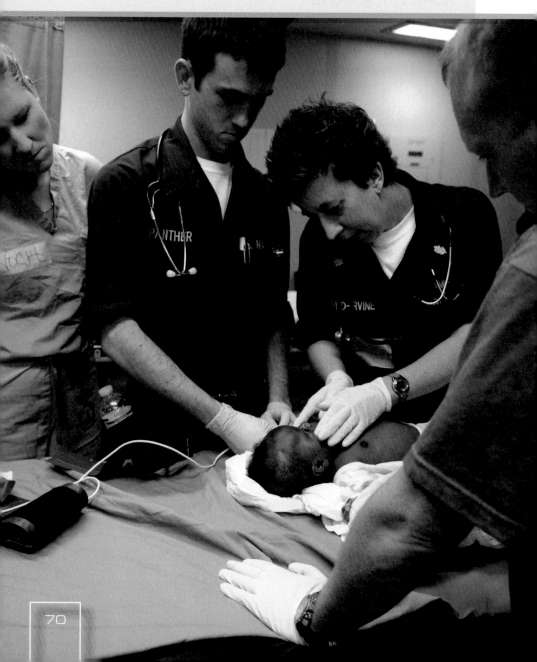

- Working at military medical facilities on shore, at sea, and in the field
- Teaming up with top health care professionals
- Working with fellow military doctors and emergency aid organizations like FEMA (Federal Emergency Management Agency) and USAID (United States Agency for International Development)

Providing medical care to both enlisted personnel and officers is essential. By taking care of their health needs, you are indirectly at the forefront of protecting the country.

Dental Corps

Navy dentists can choose from any of thirteen specialty areas as they provide dental care to sailors, U.S. Marines, service members, and their families. You will also give care to people living in parts of the world where dental care does not exist, along with helping young, elderly, and disadvantaged people. You will have access to all kinds of high-tech equipment such as digital X-ray systems. Some of the job tasks within the dental corps are as follows:

- Performing checkups
- Filling cavities
- Offering preventive care

You may never have thought about the connection between dental care and the people in the navy, but with this role you are helping to safeguard sailors' health to enable them to do their work.

NURSE CORPS

Navy nurses work closely with physicians educating and shaping medical policies, teaching others how to provide quality patient care, and working in a dozen different specialties such as nurse practitioner or a nurse anesthetist. Like the physicians, nurses serve at one of more than 250 medical facilities around the globe. The navy often refers to them as "ambassadors of hope." Specific responsibilities entailed in the nurse corps include:

- Checking vital signs (pulse rate, temperature, breathing rate, blood pressure)
- Treating wounds
- Managing triage
- Lifting spirits, restoring hope, and mentoring others

Whether suffering from a rough bout of the flu, a nasty case of seasickness, or a wound from battle, the men and women in the navy turn to nurses for help and treatment. As a navy nurse, you can make a tough situation easier and help servicemen and servicewomen feel a little bit better.

MEDICAL SERVICE CORPS

The people who choose to be part of the Medical Service Corps can select from almost two dozen specialties. They are broken down into four subdivisions: health care administration, health care sciences, clinical care providers, and medical support.

The navy calls its health care administrators the "eyes, ears, and minds" of the global health care network. There are nearly a dozen specialties under this subdivision, but the overall responsibilities include the following:

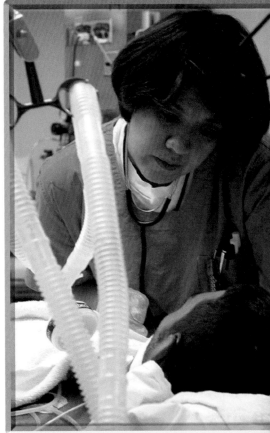

Helping sailors to recover so that they can get back to duty is a key mission on navy ships, and nurses are the people who make that likely.

- Evaluating medical and humanitarian needs after a natural disaster
- Overseeing proper construction of a new hospital

- Managing the budget of a department, division, or entire facility
- Making recommendations on how to ensure that quality health care is provided in cost effective ways
- Evaluating the training needs of personnel

Medical Service Corps workers can enter a number of different specializations, including training management, patient administration, and health care facilities planning.

Workers in health care sciences are often on the cutting edge of health care. The people in this career area are the ones that are doing the most innovative research studies and pondering the most inventive new theories. They have eleven research specialties to choose from, including these:

- Aerospace experimental psychology
- Aerospace physiology
- Biochemistry
- Entomology
- Environmental health
- Industrial hygiene
- Medical technology
- Microbiology
- Physiology
- Radiation health
- Research psychology

ENLISTED RATES AND OFFICER RANKS

In the navy, men and women are categorized by rate instead of rank. This list presents the ratings in order from bottom to top.

ENLISTED RATES

GRADE	RATE	ABBREVIATION
E-1	Seaman Recruit	SR
E-2	Seaman Apprentice	SA
E-3	Seaman	SN
E-4	Petty Office Third Class	PO3
E-5	Petty Officer Second Class	PO2
E-6	Petty Officer First Class	PO1
E-7	Chief Petty Officer	CPO
E-8	Senior Chief Petty Officer	SCPO
E-9	Master Chief Petty Officer	MCPO
E-10	Master Chief Petty Officer of the Navy	MCPON

OFFICER RANKS

GRADE	RANK	ABBREVIATION
O-1	Ensign	ENS
O-2	Lieutenant Junior Grade	LTJG
O-3	Lieutenant	LT
O-4	Lieutenant Commander	LCDR
O-5	Commander	CDR
O-6	Captain	CAPT
O-7	Rear Admiral (lower half)	RDML
O-8	Rear Admiral (upper half)	RADM
O-9	Vice Admiral	VADM
O-10	Admiral	ADM
O-11	Fleet Admiral (during war time only)	FADM

Even if you are not directly working with patients, this field is a vital part of medical care and research. What you may discover today has the potential of helping sailors and officers for years to come.

Clinical care providers focus on every possible element of caregiving. From rehabilitation of an injured sailor to acting as head of a pharmacy, these workers have quite a few specialties to decide on, including:

- Audiology
- Clinical psychology
- Dietician/food management
- Occupational therapy
- Optometry
- Pharmacy
- Physical therapy
- Physician assistant
- Podiatry
- Social work

With such a wide variety of areas to pursue, you can pick the one that appeals to you the most. No matter which one you select, you know you will bring relief to those in need.

The final subdivision of health care services is medical support. The people in this area are called hospital corpsmen and they provide basic medical treatment to sailors as well as marines. (The U.S.

Marines do not have their own medical corps team.) Unlike the other subdivisions, this one does not require a college degree. As a hospital corpsman, you will work as a medical or dental assistant administering preventive care, delivering emergency medical or dental treatment, maintaining patient treatment records, administering medications, and performing clinical tests.

The individual responsibilities of this position include:

- Serving as an operating room technician for general and specialized surgery
- Processing dental X-rays and operating X-ray equipment
- Working in the field with Navy SEALs or the Navy Construction Battalion or being assigned to Fleet Marine Force
- Constructing dental crowns and bridges

For anyone who has an interest in the health or medical fields, there is a career here for you. Whether you want to pursue a medical degree or not, work with people's overall health or specific conditions, help out in the field, or work in a research lab, there are many applicable opportunities in the navy.

CHAPTER 7

CAREERS IN ENGINEERING AND APPLIED SCIENCE

P erhaps you enjoy working with your hands? Do you like to see blueprints turn into actual buildings or diagrams turn into working engines? Does it sound like it would be fun to construct an airfield? A career in the navy's engineering and applied science area might be a great match for you. Whether they are repairing a damaged weapon guidance system or rebuilding a generator after a natural disaster, these men and women are critical to the armed forces.

CIVIL ENGINEERING

For those with a degree in civil, mechanical, or electrical engineering or architecture (or in the process of getting one), civil engineering is a natural career path within the navy. As a part of the Navy Civil Engineer Corps, you would work in the following:

- Contract management: In this position, you are the main liaison between the navy and civilian contractors. You will most likely be given the job of managing contracts worth hundreds of millions of dollars, so this position carries enormous responsibility.
- Public works: You are in charge of any of the hundreds of navy shore facilities, which can vary in size from a single building to an entire city! This area includes supervising and maintaining utilities, overseeing construction and repair, managing budgets, approving public works plans, and providing services to ships in port.
- Construction battalions: If you are good at managing others, this might be the best choice for you. You will command up to six hundred workers as they build airfields, bridges, ports, or buildings.

CONSTRUCTION

Every year, the navy completes countless construction projects, thanks to the Navy Construction Battalion, otherwise known as the Seabees. Their motto is simple: "We Build, We Fight." Unlike some of the engineering subdivisions, no degree is required to be a Seabee. The positions available are builder, construction electrician, construction mechanic, engineering aid, equipment operator, steelworker, and utilities man.

The Seabees are the construction battalions of the navy. They accomplish all kinds of building and designing projects, including the construction of new roadway sections at piers and ports around the world.

These jobs entail the following tasks:

- Assisting engineers with final construction plans
- Preparing land surveys, maps, sketches, drawings, and blueprints
- Operating bulldozers, backhoes, forklifts, cranes, and asphalt equipment
- Installing drywall, paneling, ceramic/ceiling/floor tile, millwork, and trim

ZAPPED OUT OF THE SKY

It sounds like it came from the latest science fiction novel, but it actually came from the navy. The Free Electron Laser (FEL) is a weapon that has cost $163 million to create, but the navy feels it is worth every penny. Calling the FEL "the future of navy ship protection," the Office of Naval Research explains that this megawatt-class laser system has the ability to shoot enemy planes out of the sky and even disable missiles. "The FEL is expected to provide future U.S. Naval forces with a near-instantaneous laser ship defense in any maritime environment throughout the world," says the program manager Quentin Saulter in an article by Leslie Horn on PCMag.com. The first prototype of this high-tech weapon will be ready for testing in 2018.

- Installing/operating/repairing heating and cooling systems, power production, electrical distribution and plumbing systems

To see more of what Seabees are working on, check out the U.S. Naval Construction Force Web site at http://www.seabee.navy.mil.

ELECTRONICS

The navy depends on some of the latest and most complex electronic systems in the world. These systems are installed in ships, submarines, and aircraft.

A sonar technician and machinist work on a torpedo that will be stored on a submarine. Electronics in the navy include many kinds of systems, from the simplest electrical equipment to the most advanced tactical system in existence.

To rely on these systems, the navy needs highly trained specialists. Although no college degree is required in this subdivision, electronics does call for experts in electrical, engineering, computer, and aerospace fields.

General duties of this position include providing communications support to the fleet, repairing and calibrating precision electronic equipment, and testing, installing, and maintaining aircraft instruments and electrical equipment. There are three specific fields that electronics experts can pursue:

Fire control technicians: People in this field operate, test, and maintain submarine combat control systems, with a strong focus on weaponry, including torpedoes, cruise missiles, and nuclear missiles.

Sonar technicians, submarine: People in this position specialize in underwater acoustic technologies, with an emphasis on maintaining the submarine's highly classified sonar hardware.

Electronics technicians: These people install, administer, and maintain onboard communications and navigation systems, with an emphasis on submarine navigation and radio equipment, systems, and programs.

MECHANICAL AND INDUSTRIAL TECHNOLOGY

As the navy reports on its Web site, "Without the skills of those working in the mechanical and industrial technology field, the navy's technologically advanced machinery and equipment would be little more than a mass of wires and metal." In this subdivision, you will work on a huge variety of machines, vehicles, and systems. You will be called when a repair is needed—on virtually anything!

The specific duties for this position include:

- Testing, installing, and maintaining a wide range of aircraft instruments and electrical equipment, including generators, motors, and lighting systems
- Maintaining aircraft fuselages, wings, fixed and movable surfaces, airfoils, regular seats, wheels and tires, and controls and mechanisms
- Repairing and maintaining heavy construction and automotive equipment
- Installing, operating, and repairing heating, piping, ventilation, and air-conditioning systems
- Operating and maintaining hydraulic power plants, steam generators, hoists and cylinders, oxygen generators, atmosphere control equipment, refrigeration systems, diesel engines, and pressurized air systems

If there is a handyman-type position within the navy, this is it! You will know how to do a little of everything on an extensive variety of machines and equipment. Prepare to be busy!

METEOROLOGY AND OCEANOGRAPHY

From weather balloons to ocean floors, wind speed to ocean waves, the people who select this navy subdivision as a career learn about the world around them

Staff members at the Naval Aviation Forecast Center at Naval Station Norfolk in Virginia analyze weather patterns, including temperatures, cloud conditions, wind speed and direction, dew points, and atmospheric pressure for naval pilots.

and apply that information to help the fleet. For the position of aerographer's mate, no college degree is required. You will help guide ships and aircraft based on weather predictions and ocean conditions. You will warn sailors of dangerous weather and prepare charts and maps for navigating or, in emergency cases, for search and rescue efforts.

Specific responsibilities include the following:

- Directing personnel who gather oceanographic and weather data

EXPLOSIVE ORDNANCE DISPOSAL TECHNICIAN

For those people who live on adrenaline and have nerves of steel, there is the position of explosive ordnance disposal (EOD) technician. You will be trained to handle all kinds of weapons, including chemical, biological, and nuclear. In this position, you will be in charge of locating, identifying, neutralizing, recovering, and disposing of bombs, such as sea mines, torpedoes, and depth charges. You will work with other Special Operations units (Navy SEALs, Army Special Forces, and Marine Expeditionary Units), as well as with the U.S. Secret Service to protect the president of the United States and other officials. In addition, EODs provide support to the U.S. Department of Homeland Security, the Federal Bureau of Investigation (FBI), local police bomb squads, and more. You will also help protect people at large public events such as the Olympics.

This technician position does not require a college degree. Instead, you will attend a year of specialized training. The particular responsibilities of this dangerous job include the following:

- Carrying out the demolition of hazardous munitions, pyrotechnics, and outdated explosives
- Performing underwater location and identification of foreign and domestic ordnance
- Working with cutting-edge technology to remotely disable unsafe ordnance
- Performing parachute/helicopter insertion operations

- Supporting military and civilian law enforcement agencies
- Executing underwater mine countermeasure operations to clear waterways

- Collecting information about ocean currents for military operations or ice conditions in ocean shipping lanes
- Preparing up-to-date weather maps
- Taking readings of barometric pressure, temperature, humidity, and sea conditions
- Operating radio equipment to receive information from satellites
- Operating and maintaining electrical power generators

This job requires you to know a great deal about nature and its effect on people and machinery. It is the right fit for a person who is fascinated by the world's climate and weather and the biological and physical processes of the sea.

SURFACE WARFARE OFFICER

The navy certainly has some of the most powerful and technically sophisticated ships in the world and being

Learning to shoot a GAUSE-17/A Gatling gun at floating targets from aboard a guided missile cruiser is one of the many training exercises in surface warfare conducted in the navy.

at the helm of one of them can be an amazing experience. Surface warfare officers (SWO) have a four-year college degree. SWOs are typically in charge of all personnel operations aboard navy vessels, including aircraft carriers, cruisers, destroyers, amphibious warfare ships, mine warfare ships, and frigates. You will manage all computer displays and provide full support to others through navy expeditionary force missions. Some SWOs are specifically in charge of nuclear aircraft carriers and are described in the chapter on nuclear energy.

The SWOs are responsible for the following:

- Providing air defense from aircraft carriers
- Providing ship attack and defense measures with fire power capabilities
- Embarking and transporting vehicles, cargo, and troops
- Providing combatant ships with fuel, ammunition, food, and supplies
- Providing repair, maintenance, and rescue capabilities
- Mining warfare forces, detecting, identifying, and neutralizing threats to maritime forces from hostile use of mines

All of those hours you spent learning how to play games and plan strategy on computers may be helpful in this field. You will use a computer to keep the fleet supplied, maintained, and ready to head off at a moment's notice.

The engineering and applied science division of the navy gives men and women the chance to utilize high-tech equipment, as well as swing a hammer or check a thermometer. If you excelled at science in school and loved doing shop and lab experiments, this division is the one to investigate further.

CHAPTER 8

CAREERS IN INFORMATION AND TECHNOLOGY

I f you're a computer geek and know more about the internal hardware of your computer than you do the inside of your own body, this may be the field you would enjoy the most. The world's most advanced technology is here—so get ready to put your passion for computers and other equipment to work for you.

COMPUTER SCIENCE

You haven't seen what computers can do until you see how they function in the navy. You will not need a college degree to be an information technology (IT) professional. Some of the responsibilities you will have in computer science include:

- Evaluating intercepted radar signals to figure out where they are coming from

Collecting sonar data from underwater vehicles is one of the jobs performed at the Naval Sea Systems Command (NAVSEA) in Panama City, Florida. This sailor is searching for the *Alligator*, the U.S. Navy's first submarine, which was active during the American Civil War and which now lies somewhere on the bottom of the Atlantic Ocean off Cape Hatteras.

- Identifying sounds made by ships, torpedoes, submarines, and sonar transmissions—or just creatures under the water
- Tracking surface and subsurface targets
- Operating underwater communications equipment

This is a direction of computer knowledge you may never have considered before. Give it some thought—you might be astonished at what navy computers and you can do together!

INFORMATIONAL TECHNOLOGY

With those superior keyboarding skills, you can also be put to use in informational technology. You will work closely on maintaining U.S. national security and learning all the ways to prevent any hacker in the world from compromising the country's communications. Specific duties for this field include the following:

- Writing programs to handle data for an array of applications
- Operating and coordinating automated networks, data links, and circuits
- Applying diagnostic, corrective, and recovery techniques to information systems
- Collecting and analyzing communication signals
- Providing telecommunications and computer-related training and assistance
- Performing preventive and corrective maintenance on cutting-edge equipment
- Operating and maintaining a global satellite tele-communications system

Imagine taking your skill with computers and putting it to work in an area like informational technology. The keystrokes you make could change

If you become part of the navy's telecommunications team, you might find yourself in Hawaii assembling an antenna like this one, which is used for communicating with small boats.

the course of a naval mission or send a message out across space by satellite.

TELECOMMUNICATIONS

Keeping people in touch with one another is imperative—especially in an armed service like the U.S. Navy. If you work in telecommunications, keeping everyone informed and up-to-date will be your main goal. You might do it by creating an overseas phone network or installing a complex computer network. Navy telecommunications network engineers use everything from mapping and navigation devices to classified coding and decoding machines.

Specific responsibilities involve the following:

- Maintaining television systems
- Installing telephones and other communications circuits, boxes, switchboards, and bell-buzzer systems
- Preparing and interpreting blueprints, wiring diagrams, and sketches
- Maintaining and repairing navigation equipment
- Working as a computer systems analyst, systems or software programmer, or computer network technician

Computers are an essential part of every business and enterprise today, and that includes the branches of the armed forces. Your passion for and expertise in informational technology combined with a computer keyboard at your fingertips could create the ideal job for you in the navy.

INTELLIGENCE

How well can you keep a secret? The answer to that question is important if you want to be part of the navy's intelligence community. The navy refers to these people as its "heart of strategy and operation." The men and women who work in this division are dealing with top-secret information in the navy. The

A POSTHUMOUS AWARD

Michael Patrick Murphy is continuing to inspire sailors and officers even though he died on June 28, 2005. A Navy SEAL, "Murph" was awarded the Medal of Honor, the country's highest decoration for his bravery in action in Afghanistan. He was also given the Silver Star and the Purple Heart. While in Afghanistan, Murphy and his unit were surrounded by Taliban forces. Murphy deliberately stood in the line of fire to communicate his location to headquarters and get help for his unit. He was killed in the process.

Since his death, Murphy has had both a post office and a park named after him, as well as a ship. A portrait of him was created and currently hangs in the MEPS in New York City.

intelligence field demands the highest level of security clearance because the data is often vital to national security. Does this division sound exciting to you?

Data may come in from satellite images, Internet chatter, or military and spy reports. You will handle classified documents and learn to take important data and quickly pass along the highlights to those that need them. You will need a college degree for this position, and you will attend Officer Candidate School and then a five-month course on electronic, antisubmarine, antisurface, antiair, amphibious, and strike warfare, counterintelligence, strategic intelligence, air defense analysis, and combat mission planning.

Some of the responsibilities that are part of this top-secret level job include:

- Tracking targets
- Operating underwater communications equipment
- Defending ships against inbound threats, including antiship missiles
- Analyzing intelligence
- Maintaining Combat Information Center displays
- Operating and maintaining global positioning systems (GPS)
- Working with classified materials
- Providing technical support to deployed units
- Operating electronic radio receivers
- Operating state-of-the-art computer equipment

This job is for people who watch spy movies and imagine themselves in the main role. It requires the ability to keep secrets and remain calm and even-tempered no matter what information is given to you.

INFORMATION WARFARE

Under the information warfare subdivision, if this is your career choice, you work as a navy information warfare officer. It is your job to take crucial, classified information and get it to service members and policy makers as quickly as possible. After Officer Candidate School, you will attend an eleven-week

THE NAVY SEALS

If you've ever seen the movie *Navy SEALs* (1990), starring Charlie Sheen and Michael Biehn, you have gotten a fairly realistic glimpse of what it is like to be a SEAL, which stands for "sea, air, and land." SEALs are specially trained to handle the toughest missions. Their intense instruction begins at Basic Underwater Demolition, where they are conditioned for six months, including three weeks of parachute training and fifteen weeks of advanced physical and mental training. For more information about the SEALs, check out www.sealchallenge.navy.mil/seal/default.aspx.

Those who graduate from the extremely challenging training program know the U.S. Navy SEAL Creed. Just reading a small part of it proves how seriously these men take their role in the navy.

I will never quit. I persevere and thrive on adversity. My Nation expects me to be physically harder and mentally stronger than my enemies. If knocked down, I will get back up, every time. I will draw on every remaining ounce of strength to protect my teammates and to accomplish our mission. I am never out of the fight.

We train for war and fight to win. I stand ready to bring the full spectrum of combat power to bear in order to achieve my mission and the goals established by my country. . . . In the worst of conditions, the legacy of my teammates steadies my resolve and silently guides my every deed. I will not fail.

Navy Information Warfare Officer basic course, in which you will learn everything from radar and tactical cryptology to computer networks and national security strategy.

Specific responsibilities of the job involve the following:

- Gathering information for personnel and commanding officers
- Coordinating information for exercises and operations
- Assuming responsibility for processing real-time signal intelligence
- Conducting computer network operations
- Developing cutting-edge defense systems

Information and technology is all about working with sensitive, top-secret information and getting it to the people who need it the most. By using some of the most advanced high-tech equipment, you will be in charge of vital communications that have the power to affect everyday operations and missions.

CRYPTOLOGY

Are you fast at picking up foreign languages? Can you learn one language and quickly apply the rules to another? Check out the cryptology subdivision. As a navy cryptologic technician interpretive (CTI), you must be able to speak and understand world languages whether you hear them spoken to you in person, on the radio, or over the telephone or the computer.

As a CTI, you will be trained intensely in Arabic, Russian, Spanish, Chinese, Korean, Hebrew, or Persian. Then, your job will have you acting as an interpreter during regional disasters to help provide relief efforts; operating high-tech electronic radio receivers, recording devices, and computer terminals; and protecting U.S. interests by providing up-to-the-minute tactical information on foreign adversaries. Your specific responsibilities encompass:

- Translating, interpreting, and transcribing foreign language communications data
- Analyzing and reporting technical information of strategic and tactical importance to fleet commanders and national intelligence agencies
- Performing temporary duty aboard different naval vessels and aircraft

Although many people believe that the navy, along with the other branches of the military, is about weaponry and its use, one of the most lethal and powerful dangers of all is that of information. For those who choose to go into any division of information and technology, it will be their job to safeguard secrets and facts, plus know exactly when and with whom to share them.

CHAPTER 9

CAREERS IN NUCLEAR ENERGY AND SERVICE AND SAFETY

Do you think you have what it takes to be one of the "Navy Nukes," as the nuclear propulsion community is commonly known? These are the men and women who keep the nuclear powered submarines and aircraft carriers running efficiently and safely. Some do it through research, while others arm and operate submarines worth $1.5 billion. In this division, there are opportunities for those with and without a college degree. Which subdivision fits you best?

NUCLEAR SUBMARINE OFFICER

Although the navy has quite a few different kinds of ships, it depends greatly on its submarines for avoiding and resolving all kinds of conflicts. Because of this, the navy carefully chooses the best of the best to be in charge of its subs. Officers must learn the theories behind nuclear power, as well as how to manage everything from communications and navigation to tactical deployment. There are four stages involved in learning these special skills. The first stage starts with Naval Nuclear Power School, which lasts for twenty-four weeks. Next is the Nuclear Power Training Unit, a twenty-six-week program full of hands-on training. The Submarine Officer Basic Course lasts for twelve weeks, and, finally, in the last stage, you are given shore assignment for two years.

Submarine officers are generally in charge of the following:

Nuclear-powered submarines are a large part of the navy's inventory of ships. The skills needed to operate and maintain these unique submersible crafts can lead you to some of the navy's most thrilling jobs.

- Operating a nuclear reactor and nuclear propulsion system
- Maintaining onboard weapons systems
- Managing atmosphere control and fire control
- Driving the submarine and charting its position

A commander of naval surface forces teaches newly commissioned officers about surface warfare in a class that is being held at the naval base in San Diego, California.

- Operating communications and intelligence equipment

Imagine going to work every day deep under the ocean's surface. If it sounds like an exhilarating place to be, consider becoming a submarine officer.

SURFACE WARFARE OFFICER ON NUCLEAR AIRCRAFT CARRIERS

Surface warfare officers spend their time on nuclear aircraft carriers. These ships are so large that they are almost like floating cities. With the SWOs' nuclear training, they are in charge of the propulsion systems. The special training that goes into this position makes SWOs one of the most in-demand professionals in the entire navy.

After Officer Candidate School, SWOs enter into one of the most difficult academic curricula in the world. The navy believes this course rivals the best ones found at Harvard University and the Massachusetts Institute of Technology (MIT). After a course in navy nuclear propulsion, officers are trained on conventional surface ships. Then they attend a twenty-four-week Naval Nuclear Power School, which covers topics like thermodynamics and reactor dynamics. From there, officers go to a twenty-six-week Nuclear Power Training Unit to receive hands-on training with reactor prototypes. Next, they are sent on a sea tour on a nuclear-powered aircraft carrier.

NAVAL REACTORS ENGINEER

Naval reactors engineers (NREs) are the professionals who keep nuclear reactors and power plants operating smoothly. They also help design and maintain them. In addition, NREs teach other personnel how to work with nuclear technology safely.

The naval nuclear propulsion program that NREs experience tackles everything from reactor physics, component design, and quality control to shielding, chemistry control, and materials development. Those at the top of their class are typically chosen to be NREs and are responsible for working in the U.S. Department of Energy labs, nuclear training sites, nuclear-powered ships and subs, shipyards, and for more than one thousand different firms that support the naval reactors program.

NAVY SHIPS

What do you picture when you think of a navy ship? Chances are whatever you think of is correct because the navy has so many different kinds. Here are the main types and what makes each one of them unique:

TYPE	DESCRIPTION
Aircraft carriers	Built for aircraft to land and take off from the deck
Amphibious assault ships	Called Gator ships, they support ground forces in remote locations
Battleships	Heavily armed and designed to battle other ships and bombard the shore
Cruisers	For multiple uses from engaging in battle at sea to ground force support
Destroyers	Fast; work independently or as part of the fleet for offense and defensive maneuvers
Frigates	Warships made to protect other ships and as antisubmarine warfare combatants
Submarines	Capable of underwater missions and operations, as well as research and rescue

NAVAL NUCLEAR POWER SCHOOL INSTRUCTOR

Perhaps you have always thought about being a teacher? If so, here is a possible pathway to teaching. All the officers who go on to learn the basics of nuclear power are taught and mentored by the Naval

Nuclear Power School instructors. These men and women prepare both the enlisted personnel and officers for a career in the nuclear power field.

These instructors teach the main aspects of reactor core nuclear principles; heat transfer and fluid systems; plant chemistry and materials; mechanical and electrical systems; and radiological control. In order to be instructors, these officers attend Naval Nuclear Power School for four months. The subjects they learn there include math, physics, chemistry, thermodynamics, electrical engineering, materials, reactor dynamics and core characteristics, reactor plant systems, shielding and radiological fundamentals, and aspects of reactor plant operations.

FOOD, RESTAURANT, AND LODGING

Regardless of what job, what department, what field, and what mission navy men and women have, they all share one thing: they get hungry. If you like to cook and bake, create menus, and help people feel comfortable, this subdivision might be perfect for you. Your job will include preparing meals for foreign guests and dignitaries, as well as serving as the culinary expert for the commanding officer, his or her staff, and the people on a ship, on a submarine, or on shore. This job does not require a college degree.

Many navy ships even have their own bakeshop, where culinary specialists can make everything—including delicious cakes!

The specific tasks involved in this job include:

- Organizing menus for ship crews
- Preparing dinners for guests of government functions
- Keeping records and financial budgets for food supplies
- Operating kitchen dining facilities

If you like food—creating and combining it, baking, cooking, and then finally eating it—this is a great division to explore in detail.

EMERGENCY, FIRE, AND RESCUE

You have always known that firefighters and emergency medical technicians and services are important to people's safety, and this is also true aboard ships, submarines, and aircraft, especially since sailors and officers are often in harm's way. Imagine how frightening a fire on board a ship could be or how important first aid is on a submarine that is far below the surface of the sea.

In this subdivision, you are a first responder that everyone will turn to in all kinds of emergencies. You will not need a college degree for these jobs. Some of these responsibilities include firefighting, emergency equipment repair, onboard damage control, emergency medicine, and preventive care.

LAW ENFORCEMENT AND SECURITY

Have you ever thought about being a police officer? How about a bodyguard? Are protecting people and

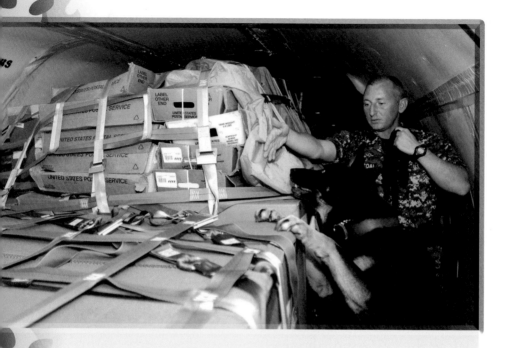

Inspection of inbound cargo is sometimes performed with the help of military working dogs like this one to ensure the safety of all naval personnel. Tens of thousands of pounds of mail are processed by naval security personnel every week at the Guantánamo Bay Naval Base in Cuba, for instance.

upholding the law important to you? In that case, consider the law enforcement and security subdivision. It will be your job to protect your fellow sailors and officers. You will teach crime prevention and offer security to four hundred thousand sailors on three hundred ships. No college degree is

PIRATES AHOY!

Looking for some excitement on the water? You will find it in the navy when you get a distress call that pirates—modern-day pirates—are trying to board merchant vessels and other ships. In early February 2011, the USS *Momsen* and the USS *Bunker Hill* got a call just like that from the Gulf of Oman. Both ships responded immediately and found a tanker surrounded by two pirate skiffs. The navy ships chased them off and followed them back to their larger ship. The navy crew members quickly blew up the skiffs to make sure that they could not be used again. The pirate attempt was foiled!

required and the responsibilities include the following:

- Providing security and physical protection for service members
- Training fellow sailors in security and shore patrol duties
- Serving as a security adviser for your squadron
- Assisting in crowd control and riot prevention
- Operating military prisons (known as brigs) on board ships
- Handling and caring for narcotic/explosive sniffing dogs

If you've thought about becoming a police officer, law enforcement and security could be the best avenues to look into with the navy. You will know that you are providing essential protection to the service members who are providing security for the country.

Careers in both nuclear energy and service and safety are excellent options within the navy. The first requires men and women who are willing to work in the nuclear field on some of the most technologically advanced equipment in the world. Those in service and safety have to accept danger of a different kind, the possibility of giving their lives to protect others. Choosing a life in the military means that, at any time, you could lose your life in a split second.

CHAPTER 10

PERSONAL AND PROFESSIONAL LIFE AFTER THE NAVY

What about life after the navy? What happens when people's years in the navy come to an end? Often they have three choices: they can remain on active duty, go part-time in the Navy Reserve, or fully enter into the civilian world.

People who stay in the navy for at least twenty years qualify for retirement pay. The longer they serve, the more they will receive. They will also continue to receive health benefits. If a person enlists at age twenty, he or she can retire from the navy at forty and get a monthly paycheck—but still have time to pursue another career.

If a person wants to stay connected with the navy at least on a part-time basis, he or she can be part of the Navy Reserve. This means that, in return for being available a few days every month, a person can keep receiving basic pay, while being free to pursue a civilian life and career.

Being a part of the U.S. Navy Reserve means that you will still get the chance to learn new skills and receive supplementary training on a part-time basis. It also means that if the nation needs additional naval units, you may be called back into service.

Of course, many people will simply choose to enter the civilian life in full. Fortunately, the years that they spent in the navy helped them develop the skills, abilities, knowledge, and experience to enter quite a few other careers.

If you had a navy job within arts and education, there are many positions for you to pursue in the civilian world. The area of arts and photography often naturally leads to jobs as a writer, reporter,

COOL JOBS

A Web site called COOL (Credentialing Opportunities On-Line) helps active navy members find ways to link their navy experiences with civilian jobs. The Web site (https://www.cool.navy.mil) helps navy sailors and officers identify licenses and certifications that are relevant to navy ratings, jobs, and occupations. The site also provides details on how to fill the gaps between navy training and civilian credentials.

photographer/photojournalist, motion camera operator, film editor, or illustrator/designer. On the other hand, a career in the education world can link you to a job as a teacher, career counselor, coach, trainer, lecturer, or tutor. Sailors who are involved in music can turn their experiences into becoming a musician, conductor, composer/arranger, or singer. Those in the news and media division could pursue similar careers out in the civilian world, including photographer, magazine or newspaper editor, speechwriter, public relations specialist, radio and television announcer, or screenwriter. Finally, those in world languages often become teachers or interpreters and translators.

Many navy personnel choose aviation, which can be translated into jobs as pilots, as well as aircraft maintainers and mechanics. On the other hand, those in business and legal frequently pursue positions as retail managers, bookkeepers, accountants, postal clerks, and storekeepers. Within business management, navy personnel sometimes become entrepreneurs and purchasing agents. Experts in supplies and purchasing may become shipping clerks.

What about those who chose to study legal support? Some of the most obvious career choices include legal assistants, paralegals, court reporters, or legal secretaries. Human resource personnel, however, tend to turn their experiences into being office managers, employment counselors, or recruiters.

Clearly those in the medical field can transfer their experiences into a variety of health care jobs, such as surgical technicians, dental hygienists, emergency medical technicians, dental assistants, respiratory therapists, pharmacist's assistants, and medical records clerks. Those who worked in the navy's service and safety division under emergency, fire, and rescue typically transition to being firefighters, paramedics, medical laboratory assistants, or X-ray equipment testers.

Food, restaurant, and lodging leads directly to positions as hotel or restaurant managers, chefs, caterers, cooks, concierges, or wedding planners. The skills learned as a Seabee naturally lead to jobs such as plumbers, carpenters, electricians, surveyors, and operators of heavy equipment and machinery.

The computer skills learned in the information and technology division lend themselves to many possibilities in the civilian world, from computer operators or programmers and data communications analysts to intelligence specialists, electronics technicians, and systems hardware analysts. Similarly, those in electronics often choose these jobs and the jobs of technical writer and mechanic.

The enlisted personnel that pursue mechanical and industrial technology sometimes translate their skills into jobs as airframe, power plant, diesel, and refrigeration mechanics, plus sheet metal workers, electric motor repairers, or locksmiths.

Service members who work in the intelligence field sometimes remain in the field in the civilian sector as intelligence specialists. Others become cryptographic machine operators, photographic interpreters, and data communications analysts.

Regardless of what career area you follow within the navy, you will gain knowledge and expertise from the opportunities and experience. You will mature as a person and develop abilities that you never knew you had before. Once your time in the navy is over, whether it is four years or much longer, those skills will follow you into civilian life and give you a leg up in finding a job that can enhance and expand your abilities. A career in the U.S. Navy is a great choice for helping to defend the country and build a career today so that you can ensure success, satisfaction, and well-being in your life tomorrow.

GLOSSARY

accredited Recognized as meeting essential requirements or approval.

catapult A military machine for hurling missiles; a device used for launching aircraft from an aircraft carrier.

civilian A person who is not on active duty with a military organization.

cryptology The science of analyzing and deciphering codes and puzzles.

entomology The study of insects.

expeditionary force An armed force organized to accomplish a specific objective in a foreign country.

Fleet Marine Force The combined force of ground and air arms, comprising land, air, and service elements of the navy and marines.

hoist To raise or haul up, often with the help of a mechanical device.

humanitarian Having concern for or helping to improve the welfare and happiness of others.

intelligence The gathering or distribution of secret information.

interdiction A prohibitory act by an administrative officer; the interception of illegal drugs being smuggled by air, land, or sea.

liaison A means of communication between different groups or units of an organization.

logistics Military operations that deal with the procurement (purchasing), distribution, maintenance, and replacement of materials and personnel.

meteorology The science dealing with the atmosphere and its phenomena, including weather and climate.

morale An emotional or mental condition with respect to cheerfulness and confidence.

ordnance The branch of the military that stores and issues weapons and combat vehicles.

petty officer A minor officer in the navy; a noncommissioned rank with three grades.

pyrotechnics The art of making or displaying fireworks.

radar Acronym for "radio detection and ranging," a detection system using electromagnetic waves to determine range, altitude, direction, and speed of objects.

sonar A system for detecting objects underwater and for measuring the water's depth by emitting sound pulses that are measured on their return after being reflected.

tactical Related to military maneuvers or places of actions.

triage The process of prioritizing sick or injured patients for treatment according to the seriousness of the condition or injury.

FOR MORE INFORMATION

U.S. Department of Defense

1400 Defense Pentagon

Washington, DC 20301

(703) 571-3343

Web site: http://www.defense.gov
This federal organization provides information on U.S. military activities and the branches of the armed forces.

U.S. Naval Academy

121 Blake Road

Annapolis, MD 21402-5000

(410) 293-1520

Web site: http://www.usna.edu
The academy's Web site explains the history of the institution, as well as which classes are taught, how the admissions process works, and what student life is like.

U.S. Naval Construction Force

1310 Eighth Street, Suite 100

Virginia Beach, VA 23459-2435

(757) 462-3658

Web site: http://www.seabee.navy.mil
This is the official site of the Seabees, or the navy's construction division. It explains their mission, roles, and responsibilities.

U.S. Navy

Chief of Information

1200 Navy Pentagon, Room 4B463

Washington, DC 20350-1200

Web site: http://www.navy.mil

This Web site links readers to information about being in the navy, gives a list of frequently asked questions, and connects those who are interested in additional information to related sites.

U.S. Navy SEAL

Naval Special Warfare Command

2000 Trident Way

San Diego, CA 92155

Web site: http://www.sealchallenge.navy.mil/seal

This Web site explains the history behind the special division of Navy SEALs, the SEALs' mission, and their requirements.

WEB SITES

Due to the changing nature of Internet links, Rosen Publishing has developed an online list of Web sites related to the subject of this book. This site is updated regularly. Please use this link to access the list:

http://www.rosenlinks.com/cod/navy

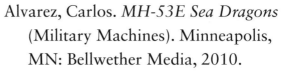

Alvarez, Carlos. *MH-53E Sea Dragons* (Military Machines). Minneapolis, MN: Bellwether Media, 2010.

Bahmanyar, Mir. *SEALs: The U.S. Navy's Elite Fighting Force*. Westminster, MD: Osprey Publishing, 2011.

Beller, Susan Provost. *Battling in the Pacific: Soldiering in World War II*. Breckenridge, CO: Twenty-First Century Books, 2007.

Couch, Dick. *The Finishing School: Earning the Navy SEAL Trident*. New York, NY: Three Rivers Press, 2005.

Deuster, Patricia A., Anita Singh, and Pierre A. Pelletier, eds. *The U.S. Navy SEAL Guide to Fitness and Nutrition*. New York, NY: Skyhorse Publishing, 2007.

Dolan, Edward. *Careers in the U.S. Navy*. New York, NY: Benchmark Books, 2009.

Dowswell, Paul. *Battle Fleet: Adventures of a Young Sailor*. New York, NY: Bloomsbury USA Children's Books, 2008.

Dowswell, Paul. *Powder Monkey: Adventures of a Young Sailor*. New York, NY: Bloomsbury USA Children's Books, 2006.

French, Michael. *Flags of Our Fathers: A Young People's Edition*. New York, NY: Laurel Leaf, 2005.

Greitens, Eric. *The Heart and the Fist: The Education of a Humanitarian, the Making of a Navy SEAL*. Chicago, IL: Houghton, Mifflin Harcourt, 2011.

Henderson, Bruce. *Down to the Sea: An Epic Story of Naval Disaster and Heroism in World War II*. Washington, DC: Smithsonian, 2006.

Martin, Iain. *The Greatest U.S. Navy Stories Ever Told: Unforgettable Stories of Courage, Honor and Sacrifice*. Guilford, CT: Lyons Press, 2006.

McDoniel, Estelle. *Registered Nurse to Rear Admiral: A First for Navy Women*. Waco, TX: Eakin Press, 2003.

McNab, Chris. *Protecting the Nation with the U.S. Navy*. Broomall, PA: Mason Crest Publishers, 2003.

Montana, Jack. *Navy SEALs* (Special Forces: Protecting, Building, Teaching and Fighting). Broomall, PA: Mason Crest Publishers, 2010.

Payment, Simone. *Navy SEALs: Special Operation for the U.S. Navy*. New York, NY: Rosen Publishing, 2006.

Rudolph, John. *A Squid's Story: My First Four Years in the United States Navy*. Lulu.com, 2010.

Southam, Brian. *Jane Austen and the Navy*. London, England: Hambledon and London, 2003.

BIBLIOGRAPHY

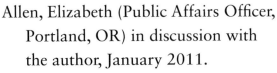

Allen, Elizabeth (Public Affairs Officer, Portland, OR) in discussion with the author, January 2011.

Armstrong, John (Petty Officer, Portland, OR) in discussion with the author, January 2011.

Bynum, Russ. "Navy to Allow Women to Serve on Submarines." *Huffington Post*, April 29, 2010. Retrieved January 29, 2011 (http://www.huffingtonpost.com/2010/04/29/Navy-to-allow-women-to-se_n_556547.html).

CNN Wire Staff. "U.S. Navy Disrupts Pirate Attack." CNN World, February 4, 2011. Retrieved February 8, 2011 (http://articles.cnn.com/2011-02-04/world/arabian.sea.pirates.thwarted_1_pirate-attack-pirate-skiffs-oil-tanker?_s=PM:WORLD).

Hearn, Chester G. *Navy: An Illustrated History: The U.S. Navy from 1775 to the 21st Century*. St. Paul, MN: Zenith Press, 2007.

Horn, Leslie. "U.S. Navy Laser Will Zap Enemy Weapons Out of the Sky." PCMag.com, January 21, 2011. Retrieved February 8, 2011 (http://www .pcmag.com/article2/0,2817,2376093,00.asp).

IB Times Staff Reporter. "US Navy Test-flies New Drone Stealth Bomber." *International Business Times*, February 7, 2011. Retrieved February 8, 2011 (http://www.ibtimes.com/ articles/109845/20110208/2-stealth-bomber-x-47b-ucas-d-edwards-air-force-base.htm#).

Military.com. "10 Steps to Joining the Military." Retrieved January 22, 2011. (http://www .military.com/Recruiting/Content/0,13898,rec_ splash,,00.html).

Military Heroes. "Michael Murphy." Retrieved January 25, 2011 (http://ourmilitaryheroes .defense.gov/profiles/murphyM.html).

Navy Recruiting Command. "America's Navy: A Global Force for Good." Retrieved January 29, 2011 (http://www.navy.com).

Navy Recruiting Command. "A Ministry that Touches Deeply. Chaplain Mueller." Retrieved January 21, 2011 (http://www.navy.com/careers/ chaplain-support/notes-from-the-field/chaplain-mueller.html).

Navy Recruiting Command. "Personal Development." In their own words, the personal development stories of Walter Lee, Petty Officer Third Class,

Yeoman, and Travis Goodman, Supply Corps Officer, Lieutenant Commander (Select). Retrieved January 21, 2011 (http://www.navy.com/joining/why-join/personal-development.html).

Salmon, Gregor. *Navy Divers*. Sydney, Australia: Random House Australia, 2011.

Underwood, Diane (Petty Officer, Portland, OR) in discussion with the author, January 2011.

U.S. Department of Defense. "Navy to Start Training Female Submariners in July." April 29, 2010. Retrieved January 2011 (http://www.defense.gov/news/newsarticle.aspx?id=58969).

U.S. Naval Academy. "Daily Schedule." Retrieved January 24, 2011 (http://www.usna.edu/schedule.htm).

U.S. Navy. "Introduction to Naval Special Warfare." Retrieved January 26, 2011 (http://www.sealchallenge.Navy.mil/seal/default.aspx).

U.S. Navy. "United States Navy SEALs Creed." Retrieved January 26, 2011 (http://www.sealchallenge.Navy.mil/seal/PDF/Seal.Creed.pdf).

U.S. Navy Seabees. "First Naval Construction Division Strategic Plan." 2011. Retrieved January 22, 2011 (www.public.Navy.mil/usff/1NCD/Documents/Strategi%20Plan.pdf).

ABOUT THE AUTHOR

Tamra Orr is a writer who lives in the Pacific Northwest. She is the author of numerous nonfiction books for readers of all ages, including *USMC Reconnaissance Battalions*, *USMC Special Reaction Teams*, and *Your Career in the Coast Guard* for teens. She graduated from Ball State University in Indiana.

PHOTO CREDITS

U.S. Navy photos: cover MC1c L.A. Shively; cover and p. 1 (inset left) MCS Anna Wade; cover and p. 1 (inset center) PH Airman Ryan J. Restvedt; cover and p. 1 (inset right) MC3c Jeremiah Mills; back cover MC3c Kevin J. Steinberg; p. 3 MC1c Grant P. Ammon; p. 5 PH1c Alan D. Monyelle; p. 9 MC2c Rafael Figueroa Medina; p. 12 PH Airman Randall Damm; p. 21 MC1c Anastasia Puscian; p. 23 CMC Anthony Briggs Jr.; p. 28 CMC Lucy M. Quinn; p. 31 PM2c Aaron Ansarov; p. 33 PM2c Scott Taylor; p. 36 MC3c Matthew Bookwalter; p. 39 MC1c Chad J. McNeeley; p. 43 MCS Rosa A. Arzola; p. 46 MCS Ryan McLearnon; p. 52 MC3c Peter Merrill; p. 61 MCS Matthew Patton; p. 66 MC2c Brian Morales; p. 70 MC2c Chelsea Kennedy; p. 73 JOS Erica Mater; p. 80 JO1c Joseph Krypel; p. 82 MC1c Todd A. Schaffer; p. 85 MC2c Ron Kuzlik; p. 88 PH3c Todd Frantom; p. 91 John F. Williams; p. 93 MC1c Michael R. McCormick; p. 101 Paul Farley; p. 102 MC1c Elena Pence; p. 106 MCS Michael Smevog; p. 108 MC1c David P. Coleman; p. 112 JOS Matthew D. Leistikow; training exercise interior background image MC2c Mark Logico.

Other photos and graphics: p. 1 Greg Mathieson/Mai/Time & Life Pictures/Getty Images; p. 15 © www.istockphoto.com/Arthur Kwiatkowski; p. 58 U.S. Army photo by Pfc. Jason Adolpson; remaining interior background images Shutterstock.com.

Designer: Les Kanturek; Editor: Kathy Kuhtz Campbell; Photo Researcher: Karen Huang